THE WESTERN FRONT

THE WESTERN FRONT

*Battlefields, Memorials and
Cemeteries of the First World War*

MARCEL BELLEY

UNIFORM

This edition first published by Uniform
an imprint of Unicorn Publishing Group

Unicorn Publishing Group
101 Wardour Street
London W1F 0UG

© Unicorn Publishing Group, 2017
www.unicornpublishing.org

A catalogue record for this book is available
from the British Library

ISBN 978-1-910500-67-5

Printed and bound in Spain

ACKNOWLEDGEMENTS

All photographs by Marcel Belley and Tom Curry.

Thanks to Reena and Neil.

CONTENTS

MAP OF THE WESTERN FRONT

Strait
of Dover

● Antwerp

● Vladslo

● Calais

Ypres ● ● Passchendaele

BELGIUM

N
W E
S

Vimy ●
Arras ●
● Cambrai

Albert ● ● Thiepval

● Amiens ● Villers-Bretonneaux

FRANCE

Soissons ●

Verdun ●

● Meaux ● Chateau-Thierry

● Paris

St. Mihiel ●

INTRODUCTION

At 11:00 a.m., November 11, 1918, the guns on the Western Front fell silent. The Great War was over.

Immense battles had been fought on other fronts – Russia, Italy, Turkey, Palestine – but it was on this jagged line running 700 kilometers from the Belgian coast to the Swiss border where the bulk of the dying took place and it was here that the outcome of the War was decided. Scattered throughout this wasteland of trenches, shell holes, and barbed wire, lay the graves where the soldiers of Belgium, France, Britain and her dominions, Germany and America had fallen. Hundreds of thousands of missing bodies were mixed into this morass, pulverized by years of industrial warfare.

The loss of life was unprecedented and overwhelmed the armies and nations involved. Not including civilians, the War's 9,500,000 military deaths were comparable to the sinking of the Titanic occurring four times a day, every day, for over four years. This war was unique among the countless others in Europe that preceded it in that, although it began with professional armies, it soon was fought by citizen armies numbering in the millions. The dead were no longer soldiers in 'some far-flung forgotten field'. This war left entire nations grieving as one, and the governments who had somehow allowed it to happen were struggling with how to put some meaning to the slaughter, and to offer some dignity to the fallen.

It's difficult to find a satisfactory justification for the War's beginnings, or to judge the intricacies of how it was fought, just as it's difficult to paint a clear picture of its results. Its history is complicated and the Great War remains mysterious. Even the acts of remembrance and commemoration were, and still are, controversial.

Running along the entire length of what was the Western Front are countless cemeteries, memorials and monuments. The area roughly north of Paris up to Belgium was primarily where Britain and her Dominions fought their war. The French, on their own soil, occupied the front from the British zone all the way to the border with Switzerland. The Americans fought their main engagements in the area east of Paris. Germany, with her massive forces, fought them all. Although soldiers from many nations found themselves in this theater, it was these four that were the principle combatants and it's the results of their efforts at remembrance that are the main subject of this book.

The experience and aftermath of the war was different for each of the participants. France, with close to one and a half million dead, simply instructed her citizens to claim any family members amongst the bodies to take home and bury as they saw fit. The government buried the remainder that could be identified in several large national cemeteries. The bones of tens of thousands of unidentified soldiers were placed beneath ossuaries with some indication of the regiments contained within. Several sombre monuments were erected to commemorate sites of major battles. One of the more remarkable actions taken by the French and Belgian people was the granting of land in perpetuity to the dead of all combatants.

Germany was in a delicate position regarding her war dead. It took several years, but permissions were given to allocate land for use as cemeteries and mass burials. The German cemeteries, designed to blend into the surrounding countryside as unobtrusively as possible, are darker places, less tended to, with no flowers. There are no monuments to the deeds of the German army to be found on the Western Front.

The United States was a late entrant to the fighting, her troops only seeing action in the last few months of the conflict. Though the battles fought were horrific, her casualties were relatively light. America had endured her own bloodbath during the Civil War some fifty years earlier, and had established a National Cemetery at Arlington as well as monuments marking hallowed ground in the United States (such as Gettysburg). Her policy with the dead in France was to offer to the families a choice of repatriating the body back home, interment in Arlington, or burial in France in one of the eight large U.S. military cemeteries. The Americans in the years following the War erected several enormous monuments at battlefields where major actions were fought by her forces.

The British Empire suffered appalling losses on foreign soil defending the sovereignty of a neutral nation (Belgium) and it was Britain and her Dominions whose Great War experience was the most profound. The War ushered in changes to an outdated, Victorian, class-bound society, and the Empire's Dominions, having proven themselves in battle, would exercise a new found sense of independence in the years to come.

The debate over repatriation of the Empire's dead and the efforts to commemorate the achievements of the fighting men caused great division at the home fronts. The work of the Commonwealth War Graves Commission (CWGC) and its visionary founder, Fabian Ware, and his determined adherence to the principles of equality at death, as well as a veritable who's who of Empirical Britain (Kipling, Churchill, the Prince of Wales), were often at the center of these arguments. This book's chapter on the CWGC explores the implications of this struggle and its influence on attitudes in British society.

Today the Flanders area of Belgium, the farm country of the Somme and Marne valleys, the Champagne regions and the rolling hills and forests of Lorraine near Verdun are some of the most peaceful, pretty and quiet settings you could hope to find. The only reminders of the carnage and drama and sacrifice that unfolded here a hundred years ago are the silent cities of cemeteries, the endless names on the memorials to the missing and the grand monuments to the suffering and achievements of the men who lost their lives.

Do these cemeteries and monuments glorify war? Why remember the dead of this war when as many people died of the Spanish flu immediately following the end of the fighting? Does the history of the Great War even matter? I once overheard someone say that if the First World War wasn't worth remembering then perhaps the same could be said about the Second World War, or Korea, or the First Gulf War. It could be argued that what happened last week doesn't matter much either. But it does matter. The world today seems just as dangerous as it was in 1914 and many of the consequences of the wars of the 20th Century still resonate in the news.

To the families of the lost, at wars end, the efforts to ensure the dignity of all who fell – to provide a proper burial or at least some record on a memorial – was of paramount importance. It was the last act of decency in a war of mind-numbing brutality. As well, the erection of the memorials to the missing, and even the monuments to the great battles, were a kind of catharsis for societies who found themselves grieving as a whole. These places can evoke so many feelings: sorrow, pride, anger, admiration, regret, gratitude, pity, and for some, a sense of unity in a debt owed to the dead. It's difficult to accept that they simply glorify war, or celebrate misguided patriotism, romantic ideals, or just plain stupidity. The men who went to fight this war were all individuals, each with their own story. Most felt they were fighting for a cause worthy of their lives. The survivors returned home, many mangled or scarred – physically and mentally – for life. They, and the dead lying in the cemeteries, or those lost forever whose names are chiseled into the panels of the memorials to the missing, are mankind's most eloquent spokesmen for peace.

In the Autumn of 2010 and again in 2013, my life-long friend Tom and I toured the length of the old Western Front by car with a couple of cameras on board. Our collection of photos is not intended to be a comprehensive study of all there is to see, but it does represent what we feel are the most interesting and thought provoking sites we'd found on our journeys. There are literally thousands of cemeteries, scores of ossuaries and mass graves, and hundreds of monuments and memorials.

It can be an overwhelming experience. The landscape itself holds reminders and scars of the fighting. There are some rare battlefields that still exist, untouched since the War. Mixed in amongst the farms and forests are concrete bunkers, huge craters from mine explosions, remnants of trenches and barbed wire. Winter frost pushes thousands of artillery shells to the surface every year and farming activity is constantly unearthing what is known as the "Iron Harvest". It's a fascinating place. There's no other part of the world that has seen so much destruction and loss of life occurring over such a large area for so many years.

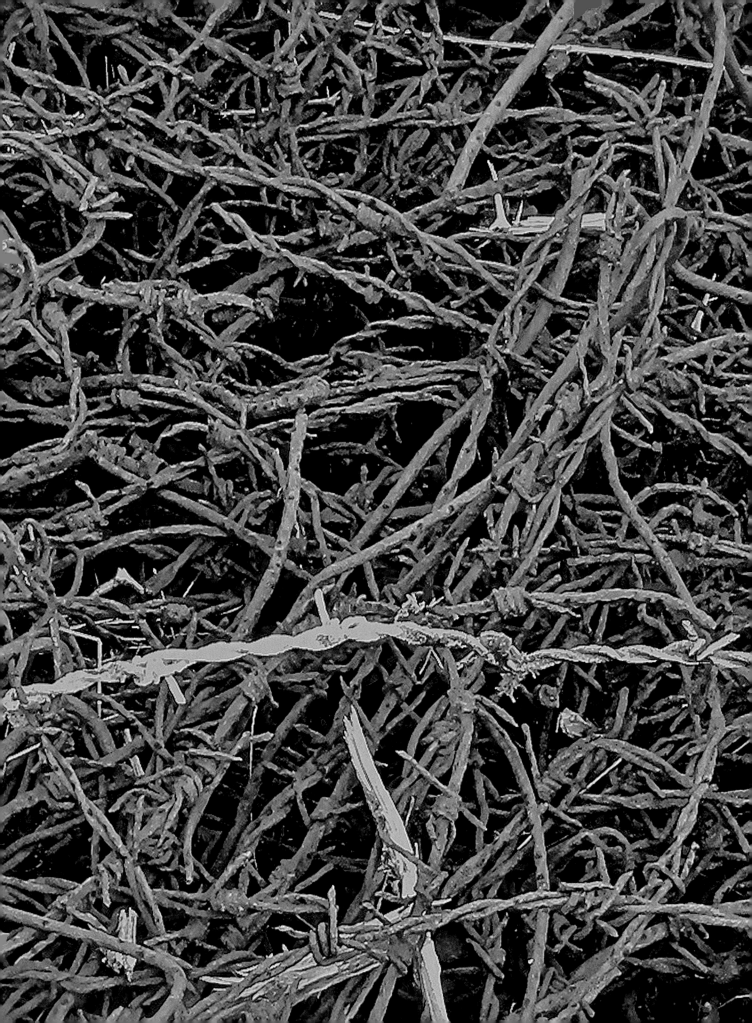

CHAPTER I
BATTLEFIELDS

IN THE YEARS following the end of hostilities trenches were filled in, shell holes were levelled, and towns were re-built. Tons of metal were salvaged for scrap and the area was returned to the farming life it once knew.

But the War lingers. It has been estimated that 20 million tons of high explosive, 50 billion rounds of small arms ammunition and 100,000 tons of poison gas were expended by the armies on all fronts, as well as countless kilometers of barbed wire. For decades after the Armistice French and Belgian farmers were killed by the score as the unexploded ordnance rose to the surface. To the present day, French and Belgian bomb disposal experts still remove and destroy nearly 1,000 tons of live munitions every year.

Some of the old battlefields still remain. The best preserved and largest examples can be found at Vimy Ridge and Beaumont Hamel. However the entire region that once was the Western Front contains other less known relics of the fighting that can still be found amidst peaceful rural settings.

TRENCHES AT HILL 62, BELGIUM

Located behind the Sanctuary Wood museum is a section of British second line trenches from the battles of Second and Third Ypres. In 1919, the grandfather of the present owner acquired the property and was able to preserve these relics of the war.

Above: Shell holes at Beaumont-Hamel.   Below: Barbed wire near Verdun.

FERME NAVARIN

Five great battles took place on this ridge in the Champagne area from the winter of 1914 until the autumn of 1918. A French memorial and ossuary are located on a few acres of the original battleground.

Ornate headstones which were placed at the graves of French officers killed in the early battles were erected at this site, only to be destroyed in later engagements.

Above: Barbed wire ploughed into a shell hole. This wire doesn't resemble modern agricultural wire in any way. The barbs are far more numerous and the main wire in some cases is as thick and as strong as nails.

Right: Remnants of a bunker at Ferme Navarin.

Reforested battlefield at Vimy Ridge.

Above: Part of the tunnel system at Vimy Ridge.

Below: Pigtail stakes for wire near Vimy Ridge. These screw pickets were used extensively by both sides as they were quieter to install than drive in stakes.

The ruins of Mont St. Eloi Abbey which were badly damaged by the Germans early in the war because it was being used as an observation post.

Above: The ground keeper's residence overlooking the trenches at Beaumont-Hamel.

BUTTE DE VAUQOUIS

Countless tunnels exist to this day throughout the Western Front, but the hills surrounding Verdun are the most honey-combed. Many of the tunnels were flooded and dynamited after the war, but the entrances to intact tunnel systems like this one at Butte de Vauqouis, can still be found.

Right: Firing hole at Butte de Vauqouis.

Battle debris that was recovered from the fields near Hooge in Belgium.

Shrapnel shell casings at Hooge.

A pile of live rounds that a farmer has left by the roadside for disposal.

A farmer that we befriended while he was working his
fields near the Serre Road CWGC cemeteries.
He invited us to his home to show us the collection of
battlefield debris that his family has unearthed since the
end of the war. Tom is holding a British shrapnel casing and
a pigtail stake. Note the massive shell splinter at their feet.

The image on the right shows another live round in the
Monchy area.

Opposite: More discoveries near Pozières.

Above and top right: One of several private collections found along the Western Front. The owner of this petrol station in the Somme valley, where this collection was found, had made a fancy display showing the inner workings of a shrapnel round complete with timer fuse.

Right: Part of a collection in a small café, near Montfaucon, France. The owner had found these items in the woods surrounding his property. Shown here are a German infantry helmet, an entrenching tool and four American bayonets.

On 1 July 1916, the first day of the Battle of the Somme, a series of huge mines were exploded. At 55 feet deep and 220 feet across, Lochnagar Crater was the largest of these and one of the few that remains on the Western Front. A local businessman bought this patch of land to save it from being filled in by the local farmers in order to preserve this famous part of the battlefield.

Concrete bunkers and machine gun pillboxes were a predominately German feature as the Allies elected not to construct permanent defensive positions during the war (their main motivation was to drive the invaders from French and Belgian soil). These fortified strongpoints could be responsible for incredible carnage and were extremely difficult to knock out. They are also difficult to demolish, so dozens of them still exist and can be found all along what would have been the German lines on the Western Front.

The one pictured above is a heavily fortified machine gun emplacement on a prominent ridge in the Champagne area.

Left: An armoured observation turret atop a concrete bunker in Belgium.

Below: A machine gun pillbox in a Belgian field.

Above: A pillbox in France with the firing slit overlooking what would have been No Man's Land.

Below: A preserved bunker at Fromelles Australian Memorial.

Belgian bunkers.

A pillbox in the Armentières region of northern France.

A shattered bunker in Belgium.

FORTS

After the Franco-Prussian War, France decided to construct a system of fortifications along the common border with Germany. The forts were complex structures which were built deep into the earth to protect troops, cannons and ammunition from any bombardment. Numerous forts still exist, the most formidable of these being Fort Douaumont, situated in the hills overlooking the town of Verdun.

Above: A retractable artillery copula at Fort Douaumont. An armoured observation turret can be seen in the background.

Opposite top: One of the entrances to Fort Douaumont.

Opposite left: A stairway, part of the labrynth of passageways within the fort.

Opposite right: A shaft for an ammunition elevator.

CHAPTER II
THE BRITISH MEMORIALS

WITHIN THREE WEEKS of the invasion of Belgium and the declarations of war, Britain's small expeditionary force was in combat, clashing against a vastly superior invading force at the Belgian mining town of Mons. Casualties instantly overwhelmed the army's capabilities for dealing with the wounded, let alone the dead and missing. Although great care was taken throughout the war by all sides to bury bodies that were found, and if possible to leave some form of identification, conditions often prevented this and it soon became obvious that thousands of bodies would be missing forever if some action wasn't taken.

There was one man who very early on could see the problem and its implications. Fabian Ware, a civilian, was commanding the Mobile Ambulance Unit with the British Red Cross, which in the early days of the fighting set up a Wounded and Missing Department. Work began on establishing a previously nonexistent database to keep a record of where the bodies lay, be they identified or unidentified, as well as a compilation of a list of the men who were missing and the organisation of the searches for those men. The British government and the Army, realising the importance of the work being done, established the Graves Registration Committee in 1915, which would lead to a Royal Charter being granted on 21 May 1917 for the constitution of the Imperial War Graves Commission. This organisation went on to be known as the Commonwealth War Graves Commission (CWGC) in 1960.

On the Great War's Western Front the CWGC is responsible for the graves of some 580,000 identified soldiers and 180,000 unidentified remains contained in more than 2,400 cemeteries in France and Belgium, as well as the names of more than 300,000 inscribed on twenty-eight memorials to the missing.

The Commission's mandate reads as follows:

That each of the dead should be commemorated individually on the headstone on the grave, or by an inscription on a memorial; that the headstones and memorials should be permanent; that the headstones should be uniform and that there should be no distinction made on account of military or civil rank.

In other words, equality in death.

The War years saw great upheaval in British society. Conscription brought direct government interference into people's affairs. Women having to work in the munitions factories eased the way for their right to vote being granted in 1918. The military's officer class and social standing were always closely intertwined, but the meat grinder that was the Western Front made no distinction of a soldier's status; officers actually suffering a higher proportion of casualties than the other ranks. As the War methodically reduced the Army's reserves of commissioned officers, promotions through the ranks brought common citizens into this stratified world, where they often performed better than their old-fashioned predecessors.

Although much hypocrisy has surrounded the history of the British Empire, its core principles were decent and it was arguably a force throughout the world for good. With Fabian Ware, a staunch Imperialist, at the helm of the IWGC, Sir Frederic Kenyon and the Prince of Wales as the Government's and Crown's liaisons, Winston Churchill as chairman, and the great poet of the Empire, Rudyard Kipling as official spokesman, one would expect the commemorations of the War to be in line with Britain's long-established ideals of glory and empire. But it's one of the many ironies of the Great War that these men all felt a common purpose to ensure that the fallen, who suffered the same fate together, would lie together as equals. No repatriation of bodies back to Britain or the Dominions would be allowed. They realised that, if left unchecked, only the privileged would have the means to bring loved ones home, or be able to erect memorials in their memory. Great pressure was brought upon the commission from the wealthy and the powerful to relax these rules, the King himself intervening in one instance. But the Commission persevered, knowing their cause was just, and also because the sheer immensity of the task at hand required some degree of uniformity.

Rudyard Kipling, before and very early on in the War, was an outspoken and passionate promoter of the romance of battle and empire. His only son, eighteen-year-old John Kipling, signed up immediately at the outbreak of hostilities, but was refused on account of his myopic eyesight. His father pulled some strings and was able to secure his son a commission as Lieutenant in the Irish Guards Regiment. Young Kipling was killed in his first action at the Battle of Loos in 1915. He was listed as 'missing in action' and, although his parents spent the rest of their lives searching, his body was never recovered. For the rest of the War and during the construction of the cemeteries and the memorials to the missing in the 1920s and 30s, Rudyard Kipling was the voice of the Commission. He was chosen to compose the epitaphs for the great memorials at Thiepval Ridge and the Menin Gate as well as the forlorn 'Known Unto God' engraved on the headstones of the unidentified. He was ultimately given final authority for every word inscribed at all the sites of remembrance of the Empire.

It was decided that all of the dead would lie together, as close to where they had fallen as possible, in cemeteries fashioned after English gardens. Headstones were chosen over crosses, recognising that men of all faiths were contained within these grounds, a

Cross of Sacrifice (a bronze longsword attached to a stylized cross) at every cemetery being the only recognition of the Empire's Christian roots. Even the unfortunates who were classified as 'Shot At Dawn' – some 300 in the British Army – would have their place here. Families would be allowed to dictate their own words at the bottom of the headstones for a small fee (which was never collected) on the condition the messages met the approval of the Commission.

The cemeteries and memorials are places of serenity and reflection. All war graves are kept in meticulous condition, from the stunning Tyne Cot – the largest Commonwealth cemetery in the world – to one of the smallest, Railway Cutting, a tiny cemetery secluded out of site in the farm fields.

Every cemetery has a Register of Graves and a Visitor's Book. Thumbing through, reading comments left by people from all parts of the globe, one is left with the general impression of gratitude. That the War happened at all was a tragedy, but if nothing else, these places have given the fallen the quiet dignity that their sacrifice so richly deserves.

Approaching the Thiepval Memorial in the Somme sector.

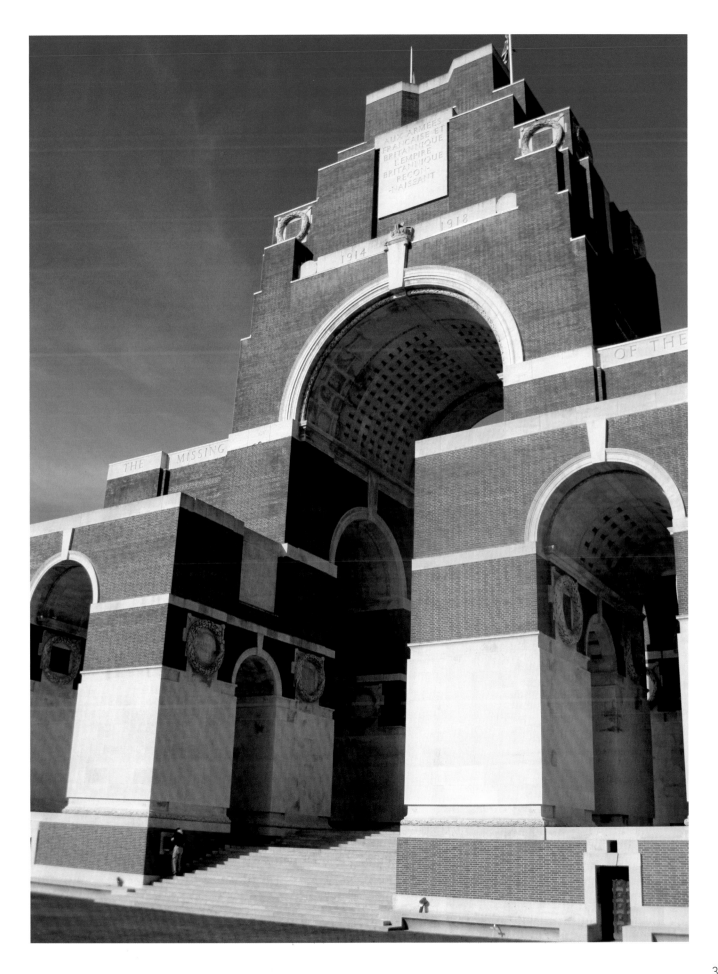

AUX ARMÉES
FRANÇAISE ET
BRITANNIQUE
L'EMPIRE
BRITANNIQUE
RECON-
NAISSANT

1914   1918

THE   MISSING   OF THE

Above: The epitaph composed by Rudyard Kipling for the Thiepval Memorial.

Below: Thiepval, designed by Edwin Lutyens and inaugurated in 1932, is the largest of the British memorials containing the names of 73,357 officers and men.

The 41st Division memorial in the village of Flers, France.

The British Memorial to the
Missing at Ploegsteert, Belgium
designed by Harold Chalton
Bradshaw with sculpture by Gilbert
Ledward and unveiled in 1931.

The Flying Services Memorial at Faubourg-d'Amiens British Memorial in Arras, France.

The Arras Flying Services Memorial commemorates 991 airmen of the war with no known grave.

Inset: A family memento recently placed at the base of one of the panels that make up the Faubourg-d'Amiens Memorial to the Missing. The CWGC memorials and cemeteries are visited often, and acts of remembrance like this are quite common. Located in the city of Arras, this memorial records the names of 34,785 British officers and men who died in this sector and whose bodies were never found.

A sculpture at Vis-en-Artois Memorial depicting King George slaying the dragon.

Above and below: Vis-en-Artois British Memorial to the Missing. Engraved on the panels are the names of over 9,000 soldiers of Great Britain, Ireland and South Africa who died in this area during the final advance of the war.

The 37th Division Memorial in Monchy-le-Preux remembers their part in the Battle of Arras, April 1917.

THE CAMBRAI BRITISH MEMORIAL TO THE MISSING AT LOUVREVAL

This memorial is renowned for its detailed reliefs by the famed British sculpture C. S. Jagger depicting a trench scene during the battle. The carving at the left of the memorial shows the troops going over the top while the one on the right depicts wounded being carried back. Over 7,000 names are inscribed on the memorials panels.

THESE ALL DIED IN FAITH

THEIR NAME LIVETH
FOR EVERMORE

THE MENIN GATE

At one of the entrances crossing the moat which surrounds the ancient Belgian city of Ypres is the massive Menin Gate Memorial to the Missing. Inscribed on the panels are the names of over 54,000 men who died in the Ypres salient whose bodies were never recovered. Included with the British are the names of the soldiers from the British Empire, who died in the Salient prior to August 1917 with no known graves. It was designed by Sir Reginald Blomfield with sculpture by Sir William Reid-Dick and was unveiled by Lord Plumer in 1927.

Britain	40,244
Canada	6,983
Australia	6,198
India	4,217
South Africa	564
West Indies	6

Every evening at 8:00 p.m. the hustle and bustle of traffic through the Menin Gate comes to a halt, crowds gather and a silence falls over the place. A trio of buglers, volunteers from the local fire brigade, step out and sound the Last Post. The exhortation taken from Laurence Binyon's poem for the fallen is read, wreaths are placed and when the ceremony is over, the crowd disperses and the traffic immediately resumes through the gate. The ceremony began on 2 July 1928 and, except for the time of the German occupation during World War Two, has continued on to this day.

Opposte: Three bronze rings frame openings in the ceiling that allow natural light into the memorial.

The 51st Highland Division Memorial at Beaumont-Hamel.

The 51st Highland Division Memorial commemorates their sacrifices during the Battle of the Somme.

**LOOS BRITISH MEMORIAL TO THE MISSING AND DUD CORNER
COMMONWEALTH CEMETERY**

Included amongst the 22,000 names at this memorial is that of Lieutenant
John Kipling, son of the famed British author Rudyard Kipling.

58TH DIVISION MEMORIAL AT CHIPPILY ON THE SOMME

This statue of an artilleryman comforting his wounded horse is one of the few memorials that pay tribute to the bond that the fighting men had with these animals. Horses by the millions toiled, fought and died alongside the soldiers. Many soldiers were so traumatised by the horrors they had witnessed that they became immune to the sufferings of their fellow men, and yet in many cases these same men were better able to empathise with the plight of the horses.

Above: The British Trinity Memorial in the French city of Soissons.

Opposite top: Pozières British Memorial and Commonwealth Cemetery on the road from Albert to Pozières.

Opposite bottom: Detail at Pozières British Memorial.

TOMMY "THE ONE AND ONLY"

Tommy Roughed it... Tommy groused... Tommy did it... Tommy ever smiled.

Left: Pozieres, France. Le Tommy Cafe sign directing travellers to a popular restaurant and privately owned museum of war artifacts.

Below: A miniature tank at the base of the Tank Corps Memorial located near Pozieres.

A mural in Albert showing a typical scene during the War with the legendary leaning Virgin Mary in the background. During the war the Germans shelled the Basilica because it was being used to sight guns. They were only able to damage the tower and the statue of the Virgin hung precariously for some time. A myth developed that whoever knocked down the statue would ultimately lose the War. During the German Offensive of 1918 the British gave up Albert and their heavy guns promptly destroyed what was left. The statue of the Virgin Mary and her child were never recovered.

CHAPTER III
THE BRITISH DOMINION MEMORIALS

THE COMMONWEALTH WAR Grave Commission's responsibilities include the care of the graves of the Empire's Dominions and, although several of these countries elected to erect their own national memorials at battlefields of their choice, the Commission was responsible for compiling the names of the missing to be engraved on these memorials, and is to this day responsible for updating those lists as more bodies are discovered. The yearly costs of the CWGC to maintain these sites are shared by the members of the Commonwealth nations on a pro-rated basis.

BEAUMONT-HAMEL

On the morning of 1 July 1916, the notorious first day of the battle of the Somme, 780 men of the Royal Newfoundland Regiment climbed from their assembly trench to begin an advance towards No Man's Land. In less than twenty minutes, all the officers and 658 other ranks became casualties. The following morning only sixty-eight men were able to answer roll call, a casualty rate of approximately 90 percent. The tiny island Dominion of Newfoundland, with a population of 240,000, suffered a terrible loss. Several fathers and sons perished together on the battlefield, as well as sets of brothers. After the war the government of Newfoundland bought the 74-acre parcel from France to preserve the battlefield. A sculpture of a Caribou is perched on a rock overlooking the trenches and beneath this monument is a memorial plaque commemorating the names of all Newfoundlanders who died in the Great War with no known grave.

Today Beaumont-Hamel is A Canadian National Park with an information centre and a staff of well-informed Canadian university students who are there to answer questions from visitors in English or French. (See also photos on page 66–67.)

THE NEWFOUNDLAND MEMORIAL AT MONCHY LE PREUX

The Royal Newfoundland Regiment has five other caribou
Memorials in France and Belgium similar to the one at Beaumont
Hamel. This one at Monchy le Preux is situated atop a German
bunker where the Regiment conducted a heroic action during the
Arras offensive of 1917.

ST. JULIEN

The Brooding Soldier overlooks the Flanders battlefield where poison gas was successfully used for the first time in the history of warfare.

The memorial's plaque reads:

This column marks the battlefield where 18,000 Canadians on the British left withstood the first German gas attacks of April 22–24, 1915. Two thousand fell and lie buried nearby.

VIMY RIDGE CANADIAN NATIONAL MEMORIAL

On 9 April 1917, in a blinding snow storm, the four divisions that comprised the Canadian Corps, fighting their first set piece battle together, captured and held this strongly fortified position. The British and French had tried to take the ridge several times suffering terrible losses on the slopes leading to the German held lines. The British assigned the taking of the ridge to the Canadians as part of the larger Battle of Arras. Through careful planning and the application of new offensive techniques developed by the Allies through the course of the war, the Canadians were able to take their objectives. It was an incredible feat of arms and established the Canadian Corps as elite shock troops. It also transformed Canada as a nation in the eyes of the world and her soldiers felt a newfound sense of independence following the battle.

Engraved on the memorial are the names of 11,285 Canadians who lost their lives in France and whose bodies were never recovered. Today Vimy Ridge is a Canadian National Park with a tourist information centre and a staff of Canadian students who are there to explain the battle and its significance to Canada.

THE PASSCHENDAELE MEMORIAL

This memorial commemorates the actions of the Canadian Corps during the Second Battle of Passchendaele.

Located on the former site of Crest Farm, it was the final attack of the Third Battle of Ypres in and around the town of Passchendaele and took place between 26 October and 10 November 1917. The Canadian Corps' job was to relieve the exhausted II Anzac Corps and to continue with the advance started during the First Battle of Passchendaele and to ultimately capture the town itself.

AUSTRALIAN AND NEW ZEALAND

Australians are proud of the history of their fighting forces and the Somme area in particular has numerous memorials to the Australian soldiers' deeds.

What is interesting is the number of cafés and tour companies that cater to Australian visitors. Tom and I are partial to a nice espresso whenever we get the chance and invariably if we were near an Australian memorial we would find a café that would be full of Australian mementos (see below). The ANZAC (Australia New Zealand Army Corps) Café le Canberra near Polygon Wood in Belgium, is a well-known stop with a small attached museum.

The Australian 2nd Division Memorial is located on the road from Bapaume to Perrone. An original sculpture at this location depicting an Australian soldier bayoneting a German eagle was destroyed in 1940 by the German occupiers (a rare occurrence as Hitler had forbade any destruction of memorials or desecration of war cemeteries). The present statue was erected in 1971.

THE COBBER

On 19 July 1916, during the Battle of the Somme, Australian troops fought their first major battle on the Western Front near the village of Fromelles. The attack was a disaster with Australian losses exceeding 5,000 casualties. While retrieving the wounded an Australian Sergeant heard a severely wounded man cry out 'Don't forget me Cobber'. That man was safely rescued and was the inspiration for this unique sculpture.

THE DIGGER

It was during the Gallipoli campaign, as the beach head at Anzac Cove was raked with artillery and machine gun fire, that the Australian nickname 'Digger' was coined. Their commanding officer could only suggest to his troops that they 'Dig men, dig until you are safe'. The Digger monument remembers the action fought near the town of Bullecourt by the Australian 4th Division during its part in the Battle of Arras.

VILLERS BRETONNEUX AUSTRALIAN NATIONAL MEMORIAL

The Australian National Memorial to the Missing is located on the plain where the Australian Corps threw back the enemy in their part of the Battle of Amiens, the first of a series of battles that came to be known as The Hundred Days. By this later stage in the war the Australian Corps had forged a reputation as one of the Allies most formidable fighting units.

The Memorial was erected in the memory of 10,773 Australians who fell in France and have no known grave.

Top left: NEW ZEALAND MEMORIAL, SOMME
There are four memorial columns commemorating the actions of the New Zealand Division located along the Western Front at Passchendaele, Le Quesnoy, Messines and the Somme.

Bottom left: NEW ZEALAND MEMORIAL
This memorial contains the names of 378 officers and men of New Zealand who fell in the Polygon Wood sector and whose bodies were never recovered. The Fifth Australian Division memorial column can be seen on the small mound in the background.

Right: BASTIAAN RELIEF AT MOUQUET FARM
Dr. Ross Bastiaan is a Colonel in the Australian Army Reserve who has arranged for these memorial plaques to be placed at sites throughout the world where Australian forces saw action. There are over a dozen bronze reliefs similar to this one that can be found along the Western Front.

Below: AUSTRALIAN SLOUCH HAT MEMORIAL
This iconic symbol of Australia's fighting men can be found near the Digger memorial at Bullecourt, France.

NEUVE CHAPELLE INDIAN MEMORIAL

It was near Neuve Chapelle in the spring of 1915 that the newly formed Indian Corps fought its first major action on the Western Front. The memorial lists the names of 4,700 Indian soldiers who died in France and whose bodies were never recovered. The damage to the memorial was sustained when the fighting of the Second World War passed through this area.

SOUTH AFRICAN NATIONAL MEMORIAL

During the Somme Offensive, the South Africans fought their first major engagement on the Western Front at Delville Wood. South Africa chose this location to commemorate their dead from all of the theaters of the war. There are no inscriptions on this memorial, rather a register containing the names is kept in the nearby museum. The names of those South Africans who died in France with no known graves are listed on the British Memorials to the Missing along with Britain's soldiers.

CHAPTER IV
THE COMMONWEALTH WAR GRAVES

As THE WAR progressed, makeshift cemeteries sprang up where large engagements had been fought, or where men had been killed by the day to day dangers of life in the trenches (known to the high command as wastage). Great care was taken by the troops of all nations to identify a fallen soldier and to ensure that the graves registration teams would find them for proper burial when possible. The cemeteries grew as small clusters of graves were concentrated into larger ones. The British decided that repatriation of remains back to Britain or the Dominion countries would not be allowed, mostly because of the logistics, and also because of the damage to morale that would likely occur at the spectacle of an endless stream of corpses from the front. The bodies of all soldiers of the Commonwealth killed in the war would remain where they died with their comrades. Those whose bodies could not be recovered would have their names engraved on one of the memorials to the missing.

When the Imperial War Graves Commission was formed in 1917 (as the IWGC) it chose to style the cemeteries as English gardens and to maintain them as such for all time. Small cemeteries would be identified by a Cross of Sacrifice and a stone fence. The larger cemeteries would be designed with stone and brick entrances while cemeteries adjoining the memorials to the missing would have even more elaborate architecture.

There are more than 2,400 cemeteries in France and Belgium and it's the Commission's mandate to ensure that they are kept well groomed and that any deterioration of the headstones, fences or architecture is rectified.

HOOGE CRATER CEMETERY

This cemetery is located 4 kilometers East of the City of Ypres. It contains the remains of 5,923 Commonwealth soldiers.

LEFT: CABARET ROUGE

Cabaret Rouge was a small, red bricked café that was popular with the British and Canadian troops fighting in the area. The café was eventually obliterated by shellfire. The cemetery contains 7,650 graves, over half of which remain unidentified.

DUD CORNER CEMETERY

The name 'Dud Corner' is believed to come from a large number of unexploded enemy bombs found in the area after the Armistice. As part of the Loos Memorial it commemorates over 20,000 officers and men who have no known graves. The cemetery is flanked on either side by a 15-foot high wall to which are fixed tablets containing the names of those commemorated.

RAILWAY CUTTING CEMETERY

This tiny cemetery near the town of Albert is located in a pretty ravine pockmarked
with craters and what were the British support trenches during the Somme battles.
This cemetery contains the graves of 107 soldiers.

Not far from the village of Villers-Bretonneux a sign indicates a turn off for Toronto Cemetery. A rough trail through fields of crops leads to this quiet spot which contains the graves of 75 Canadian soldiers. This cemetery also holds the remains of four German soldiers, likely prisoners of war who died from their wounds while held captive.

TYNE COT

This is the largest Commonwealth War Graves cemetery in the world.
11,956 servicemen are buried here, 8,369 of which remain unidentified.
The Tyne Cot Memorial to the Missing forms the rear wall of the
cemetery. On its panels are engraved the names of almost 35,000
officers and men with no known grave.

Above: Bedford House

Below: Serre Road No.2 Cemetery

Above: Hawthorn Ridge Cemetery. This cemetery is on a ridge over-looking the Somme Valley. A few hundred yards away is Hawthorn Crater, one of seventeen mines that were fired on the first day of the Somme Offensive

Below: Luke Copse and Serre

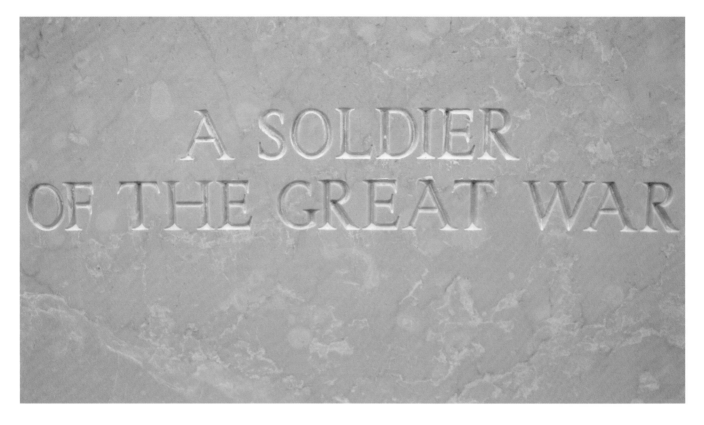

A SOLDIER
OF THE GREAT WAR

INSIGNIAS

The headstones found inside the CWGC cemeteries are usually made of Portland stone. Included with the deceased's name, age and date of death will be either a regimental insignia, a national insignia (as is the case with the British Dominion graves) or, if the remains are unidentified, inscribed with the words: 'A Soldier of the Great War' and 'Known Unto God' – words chosen by Rudyard Kipling.

INSCRIPTIONS

The Commonwealth War Graves Commission decided that they would allow the families of the fallen, if they desired, to choose a fitting epitaph for their loved one. The fee would be a nominal one pence per letter, but as it turned out, the British government never collected.

The following images are a very small sample of some of the poignant words that are carved into thousands of headstones throughout the Western Front.

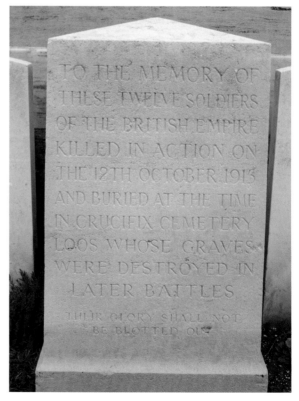

MAY HIS REWARD
BE AS GREAT AS HIS SACRIFICE

THY WILL BE DONE
DEAR BOY

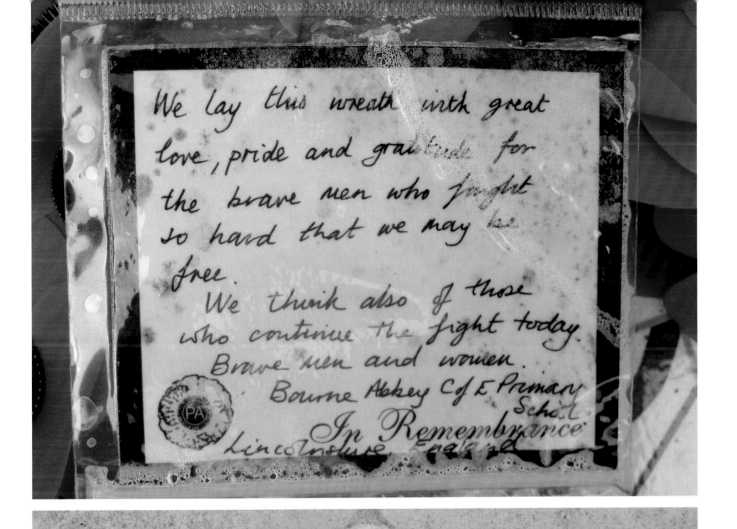

We lay this wreath with great love, pride and gratitude for the brave men who fought so hard that we may be free.

We think also of those who continue the fight today. Brave men and women.

Bourne Abbey C of E Primary School

Lincolnshire

In Remembrance

OUT OF THE NOISE OF BATTLE
TO GOD'S ETERNAL PEACE

GONE BUT NOT FORGOTTEN
NEVER SHALL THY MEMORY FADE
IN LOVING MEMORY
OF OUR DEAR SON

ILS N'ONT PAS PASSE

UX MORTS DE L'A 69° DIVISIO

CHAPTER V
FRANCE AND BELGIUM

NEARLY 1,500,000 FRENCHMEN died in the war, one of the highest casualty rates per population of the combatant nations. They fought the largest battle of the War around the fortress city of Verdun. Mort Homme was the prophetic name of a key hill in the battle. This monument (seen on page 100 and above) is placed upon the ossuary of the French soldiers who died holding this position.

The inscription at the base reads *Ils nont pas passé* – they did not pass.

Opposite: The small hamlet of La Targette is in the parish of Neuville-Saint-Vaast and is home to the French National Cemetery and La Targette British Cemetery. It is situated on the road from Arras to Lens and witnessed intense fighting in the years 1915 and 1917.

Above: Serre-Hébuterne French military cemetery.

Below: The cemetery below was the first to honour the Muslims who died during the 300 days of fighting during the Battle of Verdun and all the headstones, wherever they are positioned, always point towards Mecca.

Left: The Wounded Lion of Souville monument at Douaumont, near Verdun.

Below: De Panne. This last resting-place of the dead is the biggest military cemetery in Belgium. Many of the casualties buried here were brought from outlying cemeteries and small burial sites in the area. Here 3,366 Belgian casualties of the Great War (of which 811 couldn't be identified), 36 French casualties (of which three couldn't be identified) and also 342 Belgian casualties from the Second World War (of which 42 are unidentified) are buried.

French First World War
cemetery – Cimetière
National Français de Saint-
Charles de Potyze – near
Ypres, Belgium

DOUAUMONT OSSUARY

The fighting in the Verdun sector ground on for ten months and was so fierce that in some cases entire battalions of soldiers' bodies could not be retrieved for burial until after the War. Piles of bones gathered from the churned up battlefields were entombed in ossuaries scattered throughout the area.

Douaumont Ossuary, located on a hill near the town of Verdun, contains the remains of about 130,000 Frenchmen. Windows located behind the monument enable visitors to view some of the bones located there. The cemetery in front of the monument contains 16,142 graves. A beacon at the top of the 150-foot high tower known as 'The Lantern of the Dead' shines over the battlefield every night.

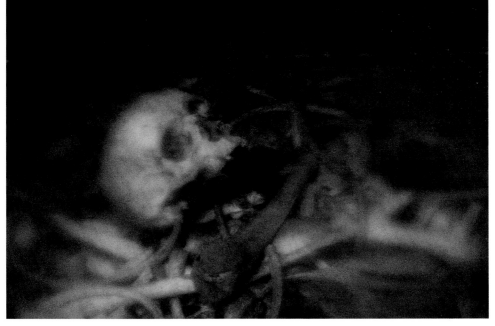

FERME NAVARIN

Ferme Navarin was a small farm on a hill in the Champagne area that was the scene of intense fighting throughout the duration of the war. An ossuary located where the farm once stood contains the remains of some 10,000 French soldiers. The three figures crowning the ossuary are: Quinten Roosevelt (son of a US president), General Gouraud (one of the commanding officers) and the sculptor's brother who died at the battle and whose body was never recovered.

Opposite: Sculpture on Butte de Vauquois monument. The Butte de Vauquois is a small hill dominating the valley between the Argonne and Mort Homme. This monument stands on the site of the old town hall.

A short twenty-minute drive from Paris is the town of Meaux, where the American people erected an eighty-foot high statue to honor the French Army for their achievements in saving Paris during the Battles of the Marne. It was here in the first months of the war that the retreating French Army and British Expeditionary Force turned and stopped the advance of the German Invaders. The French General defending Paris commandeered 600 taxis to deliver troops that were garrisoned in the city directly to the battle. This monument is the tallest free-standing statue in France.

THE PHANTOMS OF LANDOWSKI

Located on the Butte de Chalmont, overlooking the valley where
the Battles of the Marne were fought, are the eighteen-foot
high granite figures known as the Phantoms of Landowski. The
renowned Parisian artist Paul Landowski was inspired by images he
had seen of the trenches. His monument depicts seven branches of
the French armed forces as well as an eighth figure, a soldier who
has died in battle and is rising to the heavens.

Some distance down the slope in front of the Phantoms stands the
statue of a women who symbolises France.

DEMARCATION STONES

Scattered throughout the Western Front are demarcation stones that mark where the German invaders were stopped. There were over a hundred at one time but accidents, urban development and deterioration have reduced the number significantly. This one located in the Belgian village of Boesinge depicts a French Adrian helmet, canteen and grenades.

DIKSMUIDE, BELGIUM

Alphonse Jacques de Dixmude was a Belgian General who became a hero early in the War for repelling the invading Germans at Antwerp, allowing his nation's army enough time to withdraw to Yser.

CHAPTER VI
THE UNITED STATES

FAMILIES OF AMERICA'S dead were given the choice of repatriating the bodies back home for burial as they saw fit or for internment at Arlington National Cemetery. Over half were returned to the United States. The remainder are buried in eight large cemeteries in France and Belgium which are maintained by the American Battle Monuments Commission.

Meuse-Argonne American Cemetery covers 130 acres and contains 14,246 marble crosses. It is the largest American cemetery in Europe. A monument overlooking the cemetery commemorates the names of US servicemen with no known graves.

Oise-Aisne American Cemetery is a short drive from Aisne-Marne Cemetery (pictured opposite below). These two cemeteries contain the remains of soldiers who died in the battle for Belleau Wood.

Belleau Wood was the scene of a major engagement for the United States Army. A park adjoining the Aisne-Marne American Cemetery has preserved some of the forest where the fighting occurred. Various cannon and trench mortars from the battle are on display.

US 42nd Division Memorial in Fère-en-Tardenois

The Montsec US Memorial, situated on what was a heavily contested hilltop near Thiaucourt, remembers the sacrifices of the Americans fighting in the St. Mihiel sector.

This American monument at Montsec (Thiaucourt) has the names of nearby villages liberated by American troops carved into the frieze.

MONTFAUCON US MONUMENT

During the last two months of the war as part of the Meuse-Argonne Offensive the American First Army fought a victorious battle and forced the enemy to retreat on this front. A column two hundred feet high is perched atop the hillside that was fought over so furiously. An internal spiral staircase leads to an observation deck at the top overlooking the battlefield.

Ruins at the peak of Montfaucon are all that remain of an abbey established in the year 587. The Germans captured the village in 1914 to use for observation. For the next four years French artillery shelled the site which completed the destruction of the church.

At Catigny, twenty kilometers north of Paris, the 28th Infantry Regiment of the 1st Infantry Division were the first American forces to engage the enemy in Europe. Although a small battle, it earned the newly arrived doughboys respect among their Allies.

Opposite: This stone column near Cantigny is one of four similar memorials that commemorate the names of those of the 1st Infantry Division who fell in this sector.

135

The First World War US Monument at Château-Thierry, stands on a hill located two miles west of the village and commands a view of the valley of the Marne River. It consists of a magnificent double colonnade rising above an elongated terrace to commemorate the sacrifices and achievements of the American and French Armies during the Aisne-Marne and Oise-Aisne offensives.

US SOMME CEMETERY

This cemetery is located near the town of Bony, France and contains the graves of 1,844 American soldiers.

These huge bronze doors, seen in the picture on the left, open to a chapel containing the names of 333 who were missing in action or unidentifiable.

Below is the detail of a Renault FT17 light tank.

Right: The bronze flagpole base.

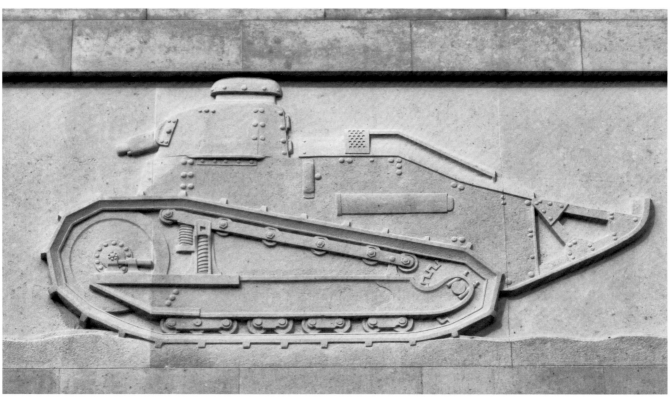

CHAPTER VII
GERMANY

BEING THE NATION that invaded Belgium and France put Germany in a situation with her war dead that was unique. For several years families in Germany could only glean information from others who had an opportunity to visit the grave sites as to the condition of their loved one's burial. By the 1930s the German War Graves Commission (Volksbund Deutsche Kriegsgräberfürsorge) was able to establish permanent cemeteries and ossuaries for those soldiers whose remains were recovered. The VDK is responsible for the maintenance of 930,000 war graves in France as well as 134,000 in Belgium. A database containing the names of those with no known grave is kept by the VDK in Germany.

Fricourt German Cemetery is located on the outskirts of Albert in the Somme Valley. It's famous for having contained the remains of Baron Von Richthofen (the Red Baron). Years after the war his family repatriated his body back to Germany.

ARNO DUTSCH
GRENADIER
†2·5·1918

Neuville St. Vaast is the largest German war cemetery on the Western Front, containing the graves of 44,833 soldiers who died fighting the battles for the high ground at Vimy Ridge and nearby La Targette. Four names are cast into the iron of each of this cemetery's crosses.

Above: Maissemy German Cemetery, Aisnes, is the second largest, holding the remains of 30,478 Germans who died fighting in the First World War.

Below: Langemark German Cemetery contains the mass grave of 44,234 German soldiers. Brass plaques embedded in the ground and on granite blocks surrounding the burial site, record their names and date of death.

Écourt-st-Quentin German Cemetery. This cemetery contains the bodies of 1,578 German soldiers, casualties of the Battle of the Somme, the Battle of Arras, the British Cambrai Offensive as well as the German Spring Offensive of 1918.

Rancourt Cemetery is located in a small village on the road between Bapaume and Peronne. It lies in fields just off the main road facing a large French military cemetery.

Nantillois German War Cemetery contains 921 German war graves from the First World War.

VLADSLO GERMAN CEMETERY, BELGIUM

In the opening weeks of the war, a seventeen-year-old soldier named
Peter Kollwitz was killed when his division assaulted prepared Belgian
positions. His mother, Kathe Kollwitz, an accomplished sculptress,
spent the next fifteen years carving a piece to express her own and her
husband's grief. The two figures known as the Grieving Parents are
looking over the spot where their son lies. (See also pages 150–151.)

CHAPTER VIII
FRENCH TOWN MEMORIALS

FRENCH TOWNS AND villages will invariably have a monument to their citizens who perished in the war. These are usually located near the church or town hall. Some are simple columns while others are dramatic and impressive for their artistry and attention to detail. Most have the words 'Nos Mort' inscribed on them, which indicates that this is a monument to the dead.

Lacroix sur Meuse is a tiny village just south of the city of Verdun. Directly in front of the Marie is an impressive monument by the sculptor Dante Donzelli (see picture on page 152). Originally from Italy, he lived in Lacroix and created this piece specifically for the village. At the forefront stands a victorious French soldier with a fallen comrade who are joined by figures styled after actual residents of the community.

Cunel is a hamlet with a population of only eighteen located in Lorraine, just north of Verdun. This small bust of a reflective infantryman is located, as many of the memorials are, in front of the church.

Monument aux morts de Péronne is located in a quiet park away from the busy centre of this city of over 7,000. Inaugurated in 1925, large panels forming the base for the sculpture include the names from the conflicts of 1939–1945 and 1946–1954 (Indochina). The artist Paul Auban wanted to depict the suffering of civilians during the occupation of the First World War.

This bronze statue is located on a heavily forrested hillside on the outskirts of the village of Samogneux, where the church that was destroyed during the war once stood. Named *The Gas Warning*, the sculptor Gaston Broquet has captured the terror of this weapon in the face of a young French soldier.

Cambrai's memorial in the town park is a tribute to the tank battle that was fought there during the early winter of 1917. A woman representing France is the front of a Renault tank, accompanied by various arms of the French forces.

BEAUMETZ LES CAMBRAI

Located in the town's square, this monument is constructed of Belgian granite and in 1925 cost a little over 17,000 Francs. The inscription reads *N'oublions Jamais* – Never Forget.

This monument at the base of the hill leading to the battlefield of Butte Vauquois is an example of a style known as *Aux Morts Pacifistes*. The figure of the woman inscribes the names of the soldiers of the village lost in the war as well as the civilian residents of the community.

Above: **INCHY EN ARTOIS**
A weathered statue of white Carrara marble stands as a sentinel in front of the town's Monument Aux Morts. These figures are often facing the direction that the invaders advanced from.

Opposite: **MORISEL**
A soldier stands resolutely on guard above the names of the town's war dead. The French people referred to their fighters affectionately as Poilu, translated literally into 'hairy ones', a term that the often unshaven and filthy men despised.

LA COUTURE

La Couture is a small town in France where the Portuguese Expeditionary Force fought in the battle of Neuve Chapelle. The Portuguese nation chose this site for their national memorial. During the battle the German invaders destroyed the church and vandalised Christ on the cross. The Portuguese were a devoutly Catholic people and the soldiers were enraged by this act. After the war the Portuguese nation provided the funding to re-build the church.
(See also pages 164–165.)

MORISEL

The artist Charles-Henri Pourquet titled this sculpture *Résistance*, and it proved to be an immensely popular series for him. There are hundreds of copies of this figure made from different types of material located throughout France.

BEUGNY

This monument remembers the names of twenty-four citizens who died fighting in the war as well as honouring a Sergeant Guichard who, along with his comrades, fell in the defence of Beugny.

JAULGONNE

This small village in the Champagne region was close
to the fighting that took place in the Marne valley
early in the war as well as the large American actions
fought near the end of hostilities.

ESSEY-ET-MAIZERAIS

The Monument Aux Morts in the town of Essey-et-Maizerais
was inaugurated on April 29, 1923. It was unveiled again on 30
May 2015 after undergoing a complete renovation as many other
memorials have for the centenary ceremonies of the Great War.

170

Opposite: GRIVESNES

Above: BELLICOURT

In the villages of Grivesnes and Bellicourt an infantryman holds up a
laurel, the French symbol of victory. This type of memorial is extremely
popular and can be seen in many different forms throughout France.

VERDUN

This massive warrior in the centre of town is looking east at the hills where the Battle of Verdun was fought. Lasting nearly ten months, it was one of the bloodiest in the history of warfare and the dead of that struggle are recorded in a gallery at the base of the monument. He stands as a national symbol of endurance and remembrance.

ARMENTIÈRES

This town's location along the French-Belgian border has made it a familiar name in the history of the Great War. The public square that the soldier faces today is large and pleasant with great amounts of activity as people go about their peaceful lives.

ECOUST-SAINT-MEIN

A mortally wounded soldier gazes up at the Croix de Guerre – the Military Cross – as the inscription on the base states: 'By the order of the Army the town Ecoust-Saint-Mein, completely destroyed by bombing, has always been worthy and courageous under trial and enemy domination.'

LE DÉPART

PROYART

The Memorial and the land it sits upon were donated by a wealthy French industrialist who lost a son in the war. It was inaugurated in 1924 and unveiled by General De Castelanau, who had commanded French forces nearby during the Battles of the Somme.

ST MIHIEL
A detail on the side of this town's monument shows a dead soldier being replaced by other generations of Poilu, young and old.

CHAPTER IX
THE WEAPONS OF WAR

HEAVY WEAPONS OF all sorts are liberally scattered throughout the length of the Front. Top rate Great War museums are plentiful and events of all sorts commemorating important dates are going on regularly.

The following pages are a sample of the various artifacts available for public viewing.

155mm canon

Above: French 75mm   Below: 155 Howitzer

Trench mortar

Artillery round

Krupp gun in Belgium

HOOGE MUSEUM

Above: Gas mask

Far right: Artillery

Right: Timer and percussion fuses

Matraque de tranchée

Italie

CAPM 2006.I.9368

Trench clubs at Meaux Museum

Meaux museum
Top left: Gas mask   Top right: Shell splinter
Below left: Shrapnel rounds   Bottom right: Minenwerfer short range mortars

British Mills bombs

Meaux museum – Poison gas shells

Verdun Museum. Verdun and the land surrounding the heroic city of the battle of 1916, is still marked by shell impacts. In total nine villages in the district were totally destroyed.

Hooge Crater Cemetery, Belgium